EDWARD ON THE SOMME

Life in the Trenches in World War I

Don & Jacquelyn Munro

Illustrated by Magdalena Almero Nocea

Published by Boolarong Press,
655 Toohey Road
Salisbury Qld 4107
Australia.
www.boolarongpress.com.au

First published 2016

Cataloguing-in-Publication entry available at the National Library of Australia

Creator: Munro, Donald, author.

Title: Edward on the Somme : life in the trenches in World War I / Donald & Jacquelyn Munro ; Magdalena Almero Nocea, illustrator.

ISBN: 9781925236996 (paperback)

Target Audience: For children.

Subjects: Munro, Edward Charles.
Australia. Army. Field Ambulance, 5th--Anecdotes.
World War, 1914-1918--Medical care--Personal narratives.
World War, 1914-1918--Campaigns--Western Front--Personal narratives, Australian.
World War, 1914-1918--Juvenile literature.
Australia--Armed forces--Medical personnel--Biography.

Other Creators/Contributors: Munro, Jacquelyn, author. Nocea, Magdalena Almevo, illustrator.

Dewey Number: 940.3092

Printed and bound by Watson Ferguson & Company, Salisbury, Australia

Dedicated to the four members of the Munro Family who all served in the Australian forces in World War I.

Edward, Donald, Chris and their father Charles. Donald and Chris did not return.

IN 1916, Edward left his father's farm in Queensland and joined the Australian Army. A great war had broken out when a large German Army suddenly attacked France.

England immediately sent troops to help the French. The Australians, who were old friends of France, joined other armies from New Zealand, Canada and South Africa.

A battle was taking place along the banks of a beautiful French river called the Somme in the Picardie area. It was approximately 140 kilometres from Paris.

Edward's ship landed at Marseilles. He and the other troops travelled by train to Amiens in the Somme. On the way, they passed and admired the golden French farmlands.

IT ALL CHANGED when they reached Amiens. There was a constant roar of big guns. Many people had left Amiens which was threatened by a German attack. Already many villages nearby had been shelled and destroyed.

Villagers were fleeing the fighting. They left their homes to walk to the larger towns. Some left with only the clothes on their backs. Some cycled while others had horse-drawn wagons carrying all their possessions. These were the first refugees of the War.

EDWARD SOON MARCHED to the town of Albert, 31 kilometres from Amiens. There the famous statue on the tall steeple of the Basilica (Basilique) had been badly damaged by enormous German guns. It was hanging at right angles to the steeple.

The two big armies had dug deep zigzag trenches in the soft soil of the Somme farmland.

When lines of soldiers charged from their trenches to attack the enemy trenches across the battlefield, they were shot at by rifles and machine guns. Many soldiers were wounded.

EDWARD WAS A MEMBER of an ambulance unit called the 5th Field Ambulance. He and his men went out across the battlefields to pick up the injured men and carry them back to army hospitals. They were then treated by doctors and nurses.

Edward and his men were called stretcher-bearers. The stretcher was a big piece of canvas stretched like a bed with two poles on either side. Four stretcher-bearers carried men through the mud and rain.

For shorter journeys only two bearers were used. It was very heavy work in such a dark and muddy landscape. At night they often got lost.

THE SOLDIERS LIVED in caves dug into the walls of the trenches. They were called 'Dug-Outs' and were dark and wet places that were very hot in summer and very cold in winter. It snowed often during winter. Soldiers were not able to wash and were attacked by small insects called lice that made them feel very itchy.

When the rain was heavy, it filled the trenches and water entered the dugouts. The soldiers' lives were very miserable.

SKILLED GERMAN SOLDIERS called snipers were watching with their rifles all day. They were looking for any soldier who had his head above the trenches. So Edward often had to go out into the battlefields after the sun went down to carry wounded soldiers back.

Edward and his men wore armbands with a big Red Cross, but the Germans used these bands as targets. It was very dangerous work.

The Australian soldiers called the Germans 'Fritz' and Fritz's big guns also made stretcher-bearing very frightening for the men.

THOUGH THE WAR was horrific for both sides there were sometimes amusing scenes. A donkey carrying a big load became stuck in the mud. No one could make it move until a German prisoner of war went over and picked up a milk can of water. He poured it into the donkey's ear. It immediately jumped out of the ditch and the army moved on.

ONE NIGHT Edward and another soldier came back to their dug-out in the rain and found that all the places had been taken by other men. He and his friend had to sit up all night in the rain with only a plastic sheet to protect them.

In winter their wet boots were often frozen and the only way to prevent this was to take their boots to bed with them.

Food for the soldiers was often scarce and they often had no fresh water. Edward once had to boil water from a shell-hole. It was brown with mud and he put in a chemical substance to kill the germs. It was purple-coloured. There was a strong smell of petrol in the drinking tins but no other liquid was available.

Delville Wood was the scene of the most terrible event that Edward ever saw. It was not far from Albert and the village of Longueval.

It had once been a forest of lovely oak trees. A fierce battle took place there in 1916 after it was captured by the Germans. They were driven out but returned many times.

They were defeated by soldiers from Britain, France and particularly South Africa which had very heavy losses of men. Edward saw bodies lying everywhere among the shattered trees and parties of grave-diggers began their terrible work of burying the bodies.

THE GERMANS had an enormous naval gun on railway wheels not far from Delville Wood. Australian soldiers would see the flash of the gun as it fired and they would immediately jump into a shell-hole. They knew that a shell was on the way and knew how dangerous it was to stand upright in an exposed place. Light travels faster than sound which explains what had happened.

SOMETIMES the soldiers were given leave to go to Paris for ten days. They stayed in hotels and enjoyed lovely French food and wine and seeing all the sights like the Eiffel Tower and the Louvre.

While Edward was in Paris it was bombed by the German Air Force. All the people in the streets rushed down into the underground railway called the Métro for shelter.

LATER IN THE WAR Edward and his fellow soldiers went to Amiens on leave. The city was almost deserted as German guns were trying to destroy it. Edward visited Amiens Cathedral and was sad that such a lovely building might be destroyed. Fortunately, the German army was driven away before it could destroy Amiens.

AS THE SOLDIERS MARCHED towards Villers-Bretonneux, they saw a battle in the air over their heads when five German planes and several English planes fought fiercely. One German fighter was shot down in flames near them.

Australian soldiers liked to collect souvenirs of the war and of the places where they had fought. When prisoners of war were captured soldiers often exchanged photographs. Australians also collected sleeve buttons and army badges from German uniforms.

EDWARD AND HIS MATES were very proud when in March 1918 Australian soldiers, in the dark of night, dragged a German tank across from the German trenches near Villers-Bretonneux to the Australian camp.

Today, that tank, called Mephisto, is the only German tank in the world that survives from the War. It sits in the Queensland Museum in Brisbane where people from all over the world come to see it.

Edward met many German soldiers who had been captured by Australian soldiers and found that ordinary soldiers are very much the same everywhere.

Mephisto

IN 1918 the war came to an end and the Australians began the long voyage home. Then they returned to their farms or to their offices.

MOST OF THEM would never talk about the terrible scenes they had seen. Over a million men had been killed in the Battle of the Somme alone. It was only after he had died many years later that Edward's tiny diaries, written in the trenches, were discovered and he was able to tell his own story at last.

This is a photograph of the actual diaries on which this story is based:
Diaries of a Stretcher-Bearer, 1916–1918, by Edward Munro MM. Boolarong Press.

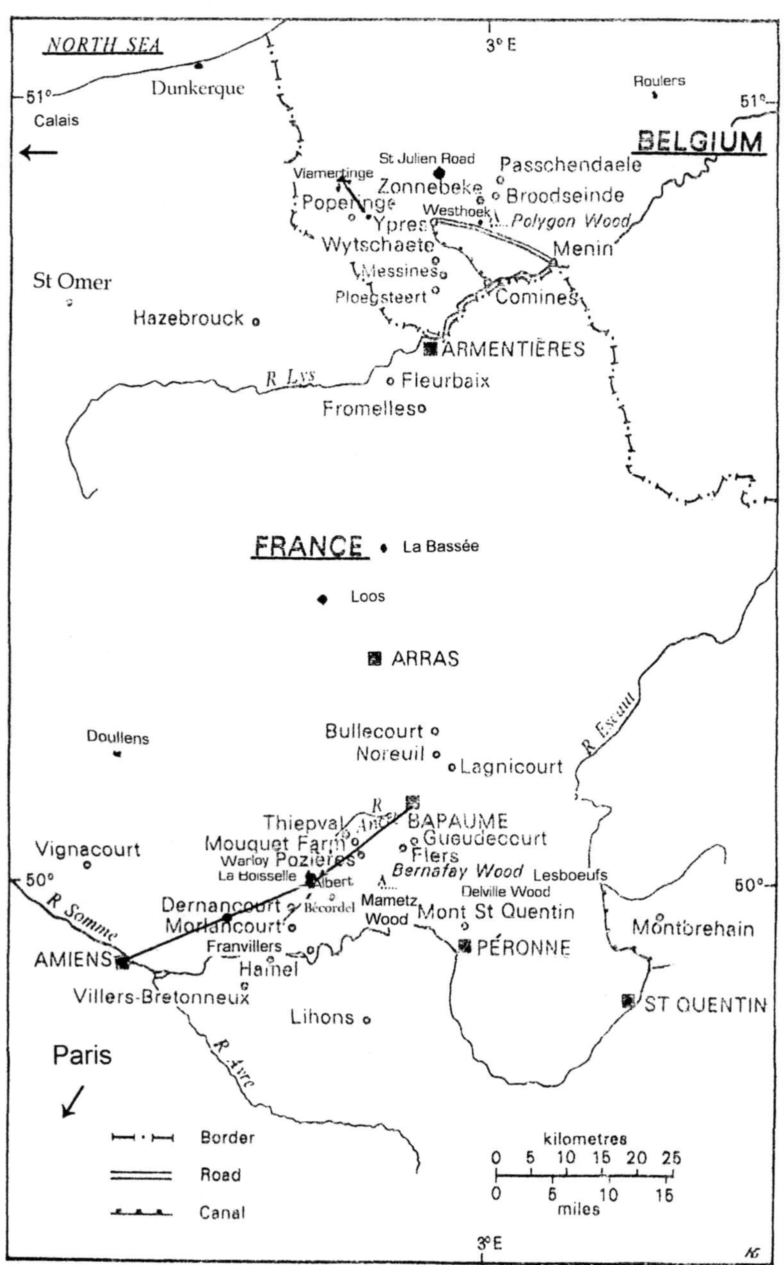

Map of the Somme area